Liverpool Fo

City of my dreaming soul
I know your ugly face
I love your inner grace
I've walked the ways
your people go:
these are your seeds I sow
city of my living soul

Liverpool Folio

Gladys Mary Coles

DUCKWORTH

First published in 1984 by
Gerald Duckworth & Co. Ltd.
The Old Piano Factory
43 Gloucester Crescent
London NW1

© 1984 by Gladys Mary Coles

All rights reserved. No part of this publication may be reproduced, stored in a retrieval system, or transmitted, in any form or by any means, electronic, mechanical, photocopying, recording or otherwise, without the prior permission of the publisher.

ISBN 0 7156 1965 9

British Library Cataloguing in Publication Data

Coles, Gladys Mary
Liverpool folio.
I. Title
821'.914 PR6053.042/

ISBN 0-7156-1965-9

Printed and bound in Great Britain by
Redverse Limited
Harlescott, Shrewsbury

For my parents, John and Gladys Reid

Preface

As a poet, I am fortunate to have been brought up in Liverpool, a city of remarkable vitality, dramatic contrast and cultural opportunity. My childhood and adolescence were spent near the city centre — visually stimulating with the waterfront and the stately classical buildings. My senses were sharpened further by visits to North Wales, beckoning on the Merseyside skyline. With each return to the city I was more keenly aware of my surroundings.

For anyone living near the Mersey, the sea is an ever-present influence — the Irish Sea around the miles of coast, its salt in the winds blowing up from the river; this, and the life of the port, with its great seafaring past. Like many children on Sunday-afternoon walks to the Pier Head, I was told by my parents of the notorious slave trade in the eighteenth century, and the old Goree Piazzas where slaves (they said) were chained in large iron rings embedded into the walls. Walks along the Landing Stage viewing the variety of shipping, and trips on ferry boats across the Mersey to Wallasey ('over the water') quickened my eager imagination.

There is a sense in which a city is one person's city: and the Liverpool of these poems is mine. I conceived the idea for this book when I realised that many of my poems arose directly from my local background and experience, and that some of the more personal poems, and those reflecting my family, were also connected with the same experience, being 'of' the city and about Liverpool people. Others were written in response to the Merseyside environment — descriptive pieces and evocations of the historical past. Other poems followed, of various kinds and in various moods. Then there was the hunt for photographs, and once or twice it was the photograph that was the inspiration.

Liverpool is the core of Merseyside, and it is from here that the strong character of the area derives — the essential wit, warmth and liveliness of Liverpudlians (a fittingly comical name, since a sustaining humour abounds). Perhaps something of the flavour is due to hybrid origins, so many of the inhabitants being the descendants of immigrants who settled here in vast numbers in the nineteenth century. My own mixed ancestry — Welsh, Swedish, Italian, Irish — is an example.

Merseyside now has the greatest concentration of activity in the arts outside London. Writers and artists of every kind develop and cluster here. In recent years a city in transition, Liverpool today is responding to change and challenge — as the immense success of the 1984 International Garden Festival (the first to be held in Britain) has shown. Like the large liners of the past, she is 'on her stern and ready to go'.

G.M.C.

Acknowledgements

My special thanks to Tom Wood and all the photographers who have given me permission to print their work; to the *Liverpool Daily Post and Echo* for permission to print the photograph of the Royal Hippodrome; to Paul and Maureen Carter for kindly loaning E. Dunnicliffe's photograph of St. George's Plateau; to the private collector for permission to reproduce Atkinson Grimshaw's painting 'Liverpool from Wapping'; and to Mark Allison for assistance with the cover.

Some of the poems first appeared in the following journals and anthologies:
Ambit, Jabberwocky Collections, Meridian, New Poetry, Outposts, Overspill, Poetry Merseyside, Poetry Nottingham, Poetry Wales.
Several have been broadcast on *BBC Radio Merseyside,* and recorded by Gladys Mary Coles for *Dial-a-Poem* (051 486 2852).

'The Plaster Madonna' received the Lake Aske Memorial Award.

Contents

Mersey Nights

O — for the night of those Mersey nights
that I remember,
and the light of those pin-star lights
that I recall
nodding on a river wind.
So little light, but motion in the night.

Then ferries creeping in
like fluorescent crabs
with seagulls crying in
rain spitting in
wind wilding in
over the black waves.

Densest dark in darkest eddies
floating by the floating stage —
and all the men and women merely seagulls
playing at crossing the page —

it's written on the waves:
the liquid life of Merseyside.

Litter

Old Man

Like Nelson
on the quarter-deck of the Victory
he slowly paces the Pier Head parapets
above the river, his cradle.

He leans on the railings, blinks,
watery sunlight
warming thin memories:
the cast-iron roadway, carts,
cattle, Gladstone bags and collars,
his sticky lollipop falling,
grit on wet sweets,
black-shawled women
bartering for fish,
his father's calloused hand,
tarry wood and ropes,
fat bollards, creaking ferries,
smell of river ooze,
intermittent shrike of gulls
rending the air, the heart,
the memories.

He's part of it all
of generations of gulls of wingbeats
of the heavy clock tolling in the tall tower
of the Liver birds, their leaden cross of wings.
He came here with his Nelly,
evenings, in Sunday tie and boots.
Trams left for mysterious destinations
(Allerton, Fazakerley, Croxteth),
travelling inside twin hedgerows
rattling and clicking to old sandstone villages
at the city's green fringes.

He watches light tacking on the Mersey,
the dark crocodiles of waves, urgent,
the river mouth beckoning
salt-hints from the sea-line
— in this his small freedom,
soon.

Presence *(Formby Beach)*

There's a voice in the pines
in the forest
guarding the stillness of the sands.
From the shoreline
to the line of dunes
and into the line of the pines,
it speaks
among the ferns,
along the sweet earth,
up the length of barks
to the blue-black beyond.
It knows
the red beneath lichen greens,
tenderness under the crust,
the seeds within the cones;
it breathes
                from the forest
to the listening grasses on the dunes,
to the time-full waves
on which all ships
go solitary
out to sea.

A Grandfather's Tale: the Ellan Vannin, *December 1909*

(to my father John P. Reid)

In gale force winds, a grey December day,
the *Ellan Vannin* steamed out of the bay.
At the Isle of Man, business completed
(the poultry orders for Christmas secured),
I had planned to sail on her, return home
over the Irish Sea, its stinging foam.
My baggage was packed for dear Liverpool;
passengers boarded, and I felt a fool:
prone to sea-sickness, I stayed on the quay,
watched as the mail steamer put out to sea.

Next morning I heard that a great wave tossed
the *Ellan Vannin*, how all lives were lost
near the Bar Light, within sight of the Port.
And now, my son, comes the shattering thought:
if I'd been brave and against sickness fought,
you would not have been born — for there I would be
with the *Ellan Vannin*, deep in the sea.

A Liverpool Dock, 1982

An empty sink.
No water, no ships.
A relief map of mud,
contours of ooze.
An opaque well.
Drop anything in here —
a ring, a boot, a body —
it will be stored without sign.

Memories too are sunk in there —
of cobbled quays with human throngs,
the clamour of cargoes, foreign tongues.
Above the mudline: 1849
the plaque's a reminder
everything falls
in the clogging hold
of time.

Pigeons and shadows inhabit warehouses,
weeds erupt through pavings,
bollards are fungus-furred.
And the river hurries by
preoccupied
with its own new silence.

Albert Dock: Regeneration, 1984

First, the Victorian grand design
named after the Prince
with an idealistic mind.
Jesse Hartley built a dock to survive —
and revive.
Functional solidity in form and line
yet Venetian style for each warehouse block:
where water doubled the thickets of rigging,
cranes swung cargoes through elegant arches
direct from vessels to vaulted rooms.
A century of storage,
dry, safe and cold.

Then the death-phase:
crusted rust on cast-iron columns,
corrosion claiming the colonnades,
insinuation of silt and slime
into the basin abandoned by trade;
blind boarded-up eyes
of the riverside storeys —
frontage to phantoms and rats.

Next, the gradual reincarnation
after testing of timbers
for internal rot:
successive scourings and series of scrapings
restore the original rosy tones.
From mausoleum to Maritime Museum,
refilling the dock with river and people —
waterspace for a Space Age city.

CLAN LINE

Liners

Clinging like barnacles,
an old mariner's memories:

a life striding the sea
on liners, Liverpool leviathans
putting out with attendant tugs
moving slowly from the mother-river,
returning through the Bar
to berth in the womb-haven.

Those shining, sharp-lined ships
ploughing Atlantic furrows,
fleets of Cunard and White Star:
Carmania, Carpathia, Ascania,
Georgic, Brittanic, Majestic.
Sea palaces, floating towns
with floating populations.
Graceful ocean greyhounds —
Mauritania, Media, Parthia,
Duchesses, white *Empresses*
of France, Scotland, Canada.

A drift of names:
he hears their syllables
in seagulls' cries.

Dredging *(Cast-Iron Shore)*

A dredger creeps in the noondark day
to river my sand-banked soul;
a dredger dumb as the world to come
shovels my mud and my clay.

The sad-clouded sky flattens away
streets of pinioned earth —
        and where lives go
        like leaves from sometime trees
        so go (I know)
        the silt and drudge of dreams.

Channels clear with deeper water
flow like flooded streams
when sludge is sucked and carried away
to sink in dissolving seas.

42

Timepiece *(Merseyside County Museum)*

Those ebony clocks ticking velvet death
were chorus to every act in sable night,
circuiting the hours, dark and light,
like metronomes measuring breath.

I entered this gallery of time
at three on a winter afternoon
to a whirring, gonging, collective tune —
witnesses of the past utter the present chime —
ding-dong the daylong grief
tick-tock the gladness brief.

Some, like tall coffins stood on end,
with pale disc faces; a rare few
old water-clocks (what urgency then in mechanics new
to corner time flowing riverlike round a bend?).

Others, in gold or silver filigree,
hold tiny jewelled mystery
made by the craftsman's hands, now gone,
while fingered time clicks on.

Time is life : we divide, watch, kill it.
Yet this, by Thomas Turner, 1788,
still sings an anthem of birth, death, fate
in the seconds of a minute.
Ding-dong the daylong grief
tick-tock the gladness brief.

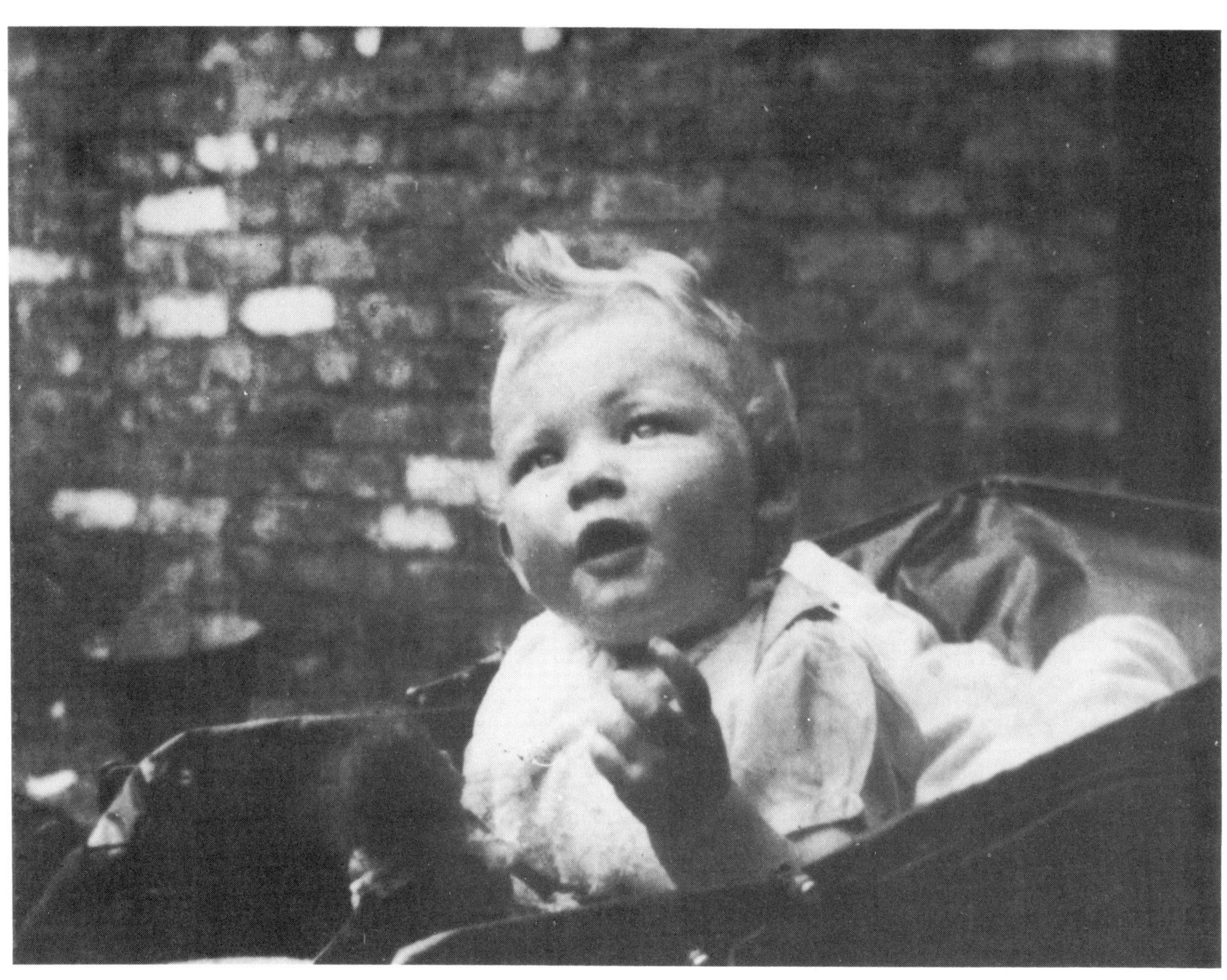

Liverpool Child

The house stood tall, three storeys to the sky,
a basement deeply dim into the earth,
wedged in a terraced row
of Victorian respectability.
The house stood dark, its sandstone wore
a century's coat of grime
frayed at the cuffs which showed
sad nineteenth century pink.
Mysterious attics high
by dusty bannisters beckoned
like the forbidden
or a winking Christmas tree to me.
I climbed, aged two,
a struggle to the unknown,
afraid to see my handprints in the dust
yet going on and up the attic stairs:
once there, alone,
unable to descend.
        Difficult to recapture
        that infant watershed,
        delight in newness,
        in waking, in sleeping,
        in simple things.
It was an adult house,
a house with knowledge
of family and times,
fulfilled, with personality.

Viewed from Everton Brow
across the city-depths
of endless rooftops, factories and spires,
lingered a distant vista of Welsh hills
faint as a mirage
through industrial gloom,
yet greenly near and sad
on bright sea days.
        Pity there was, and pathos
        in those hills, with promise
        of a world beyond a world
        of concrete sorrow,
        solidified religion.
Drear crumbling walls of houses
once pregnant with laughter,
with fear, with many loves —
those now disintegrate

clearing this ground
sanctified by generations,
clearing for new edifices
and new emotions.
Spiritual love fluting
when the breeze filtered
through long streets of dust and paper,
a breath from the sea
on quiet summer evenings
deep in the city's womb.
Discord in children's shouts, strident
across the still warm air,
across parched grass of arid parks
and pavements cooling
from noonday pressure heat.
        Benediction tolled in gold
        while dogs yelped across yards
        where fat-armed women gossiped,
        waiting
        for sweating men who quaffed
        in smelly confines of corner pubs
        but did not know their thirst.
        And the women, in confinements
        knew the end of life
        and the beginning,
        yet remained unaware
        like lumps of stone unsculptured.

Exciting on the waterfront,
great liners gracing in,
to brood in dock like caged lions.
There, stately buildings preside,
the Mersey skyline a child's New York:
the Liver tall, uniquely towered
and topped by twin birds,
giant cormorants in copper,
wings lifted, poised for flight;
one bird looking seawards
pensive down the estuary,
the other gazing citywards
into another sea.
        From early days, toddling there
        to cross on friendly ferries
        for seaside play in shell pools,
        sun and brittleness;
        later to contemplate
        inevitable tides
        and human behaviour bare,
        pathetic on beaches
        like sand insects.

I saw a street sparrow splayed
so raw, so tender on the cruel kerb,

plummeted from its gutter nest
too young to know its wings:
vulnerable
as my mother's smile,
a child splashing barefoot in the waves,
a whiskered old one huddled in a shawl
upon her step, cold in the heat.
        Next day I climbed
        to see the nest
        roofed high in a grey-slate school,
        and found a secret turret
        aloof from humanity
        where looking down
        I loved humanity
        and knew how to descend.

A bedroom small, my own
reflection of life and living,
a process of sleep and wakefulness
to mornings of glim light,
to fog-bound days mysterious,
all movements significant in mist,
to brave industrial sunshine
and sticky tar days of street warmth.
        There was a small tooth
        in the fireplace of my room,
        a rounded tooth, creamly boned,
        a tooth which set my thoughts
        on morbid paths of dead inhabitants
        and finished Edwardian lives.
        Then joy replaced depression —
        this tooth belonged to pussy,
        or so my mother said.

Swish through those leaves
of crisp brown autumn gutters,
a pang of ending, with renewal
lost from sight
when fallen leaves turned plashy
and skies, diffused in grey,
        turned into thick night . . .

Going back, the streets are hard to find,
erased entirely or become
new precincts of a different kind.

The Plaster Madonna

Spring in the streets brought conjecture
for the texture of flowers, known
only by their absence in that cemented world
where clouds, fleecing over from Wales,
held myths of scudding lamb and new-born bud.
I longed to have the scent of flowers,
to see and touch and know,
so resented the plaster madonna
of the virginal Catholic classroom
(May was proclaimed her month, blossom her prize).
The petalled offering at her feet
seemed pagan sacrifice to stiffest clay,
to dusty obscene toes, chipped carving,
faded paint and painted face
unable to see or touch or know
those flowers mine by right
of sight and yearning of the senses.

End of day, warm dust of May
moting the air, I stayed to evade
black moth nun along a corridor,
dark ghost in shafted sun
moving silently in childless school.
Disobeying the rule, child behind frosted glass
I hid, alone with the plaster madonna,
sinking in flower bliss, kissed
the smooth, incredible narcissi:
suspension of all
in the silent seeking senses.

Night flitting nun (inevitably)
descended like a bat from Hades.
In spite of cloistered canticles and purity
of endless, incensed beads,
wrath uncensored rose from
those intensely dense medieval robes.

Outcast from the flowers, no fields
no dale, I ran renewed
through Everton Vale.

SAVINGS
No time for comedy
BARKER & DOBS
VIKING CHOCOLA

Fall of a Pleasure Dome (1876—1980)

'The Hippodrome's coming down!'
I heard, and went in time
for the final curtain.
Only the entrance remained
and the circle seats
above a void, red plush in tiers
facing the tumbledown streets.
Tall walls cascade
like the falling Bastille,
an era ends, images fade.
'The Hippodrome's coming down!'
a pleasure dome descends
uncoiling the celluloid memories
of childhood.

I recall long queues, with Mum and Auntie Lil —
sometimes in drizzle, chocolate already eaten,
the slow shuffle towards the pay-box
over mosaic heads on the foyer floor
(four clowns, relic of Hengler's Circus).
Then later, furtive meetings,
holding hands through 'Tarzan'
or 'Flash Gordon', at noisy Saturday matinees:
there in 'The Gods', a high cuddle-place
looking down on Liverpool's largest stage
swathed in velvet, the magic screen.
Afterwards, the abrupt darkness of streets
(ah, shining puppy-nosed youth
the glow on downy choir-boy cheeks).

With the dust-clouds, shapes, echoes:
voices, applause from an age out of reach —
Houdini, Little Tich, Chaplin,
Vesta Tillie, Florrie Forde,
George V and his Queen —
a roll-call of ghosts.
Theatre of varieties, cinema,
palace of memories, illusions, dreams:
your sounds die as the rubble settles;
only a workman whistles and sings
'The Royal Hippodrome's come down!'

A City's Troubles

Those acid sounds
of history
citrify the air.

Those screaming silences
of the committed
null the mind

while cries of generations
are lost
under the wailing
of the new born.

Fresh hungers tear the day
old hungers voiceless in the night
creep to a tree grave.

Laughter resounds
in ruined cloisters
like footsteps
in new cathedrals.

Metropolitan Cathedral

Long poniards form a crown of thorns;
the coloured lantern glints and warns.
Inside, shafts of radiant light
stained in shades of the spectrum bright
illumine colours of the soul.

Matthew, Mark, Luke and John
ring out a sonorous carillon —
great iron bells at eighty feet
swinging high above Hope Street.

City Parks

Sefton, Princes, Wavertree,
Calderstones, Newsham, Stanley . . .

city parks
preside, entice:
landscaped lungs
purpose-built
pre-dating smokeless fuel.

Tall trees — some more ancient
than the parks — survivors
of soot-lacquered days,
bristle brightly now
in clean-air zones.

Old lads, under the boughs,
walk slowly where once
they skimmed with balls,
sailed high in prams.

Lakes, lodges, lawns
lasting through seasons
of peace and war.
Observers of generations,
the thick-ridged boles
growing through seasons
of human budding —
babies, children, lovers,
mothers, the employed,
the unemployed.

Great roots grapple
the banked earth
border old sandstone walls
reach under back-gardens
where bunting billows
on strung-out lines.

Unrehearsed, from unwritten scripts
dramas are performed each day
against the constant backcloth
of the park . . .
Sefton, Princes, Wavertree,
Calderstones, Newsham, Stanley.

Football City

The air seeps in damp clods
chill as the raw cold sods
although the rain is ceasing.

Spring weeps in clouds of clay
suspended over the day
of a city still sleeping.

By noon, from every street
a regiment of feet
to the great turf hurrying.

And soon, around the Ground
rises the stirring sound —
thousands as one voice cheering.

Nearby, on Anfield graves
earth vibrates with the waves
of live supporters' chanting.

Religion in colours
in red and blue favours
on the grass altar playing.

12

To John Lennon *(murdered December 8, 1980)*

Blackly the Mersey surges in the dark
Blackly the buildings surround the drab park
Blackly a tree sways outside the lit pane
Black is a cross silhouetted in rain
Blackly in fame his tragic fate lay
Blackly the tarry road led him away
Black is the season, but most black by far
The night sky in winter, without John or a star

"Liverpool is the 'pool of life'" Carl G. Jung

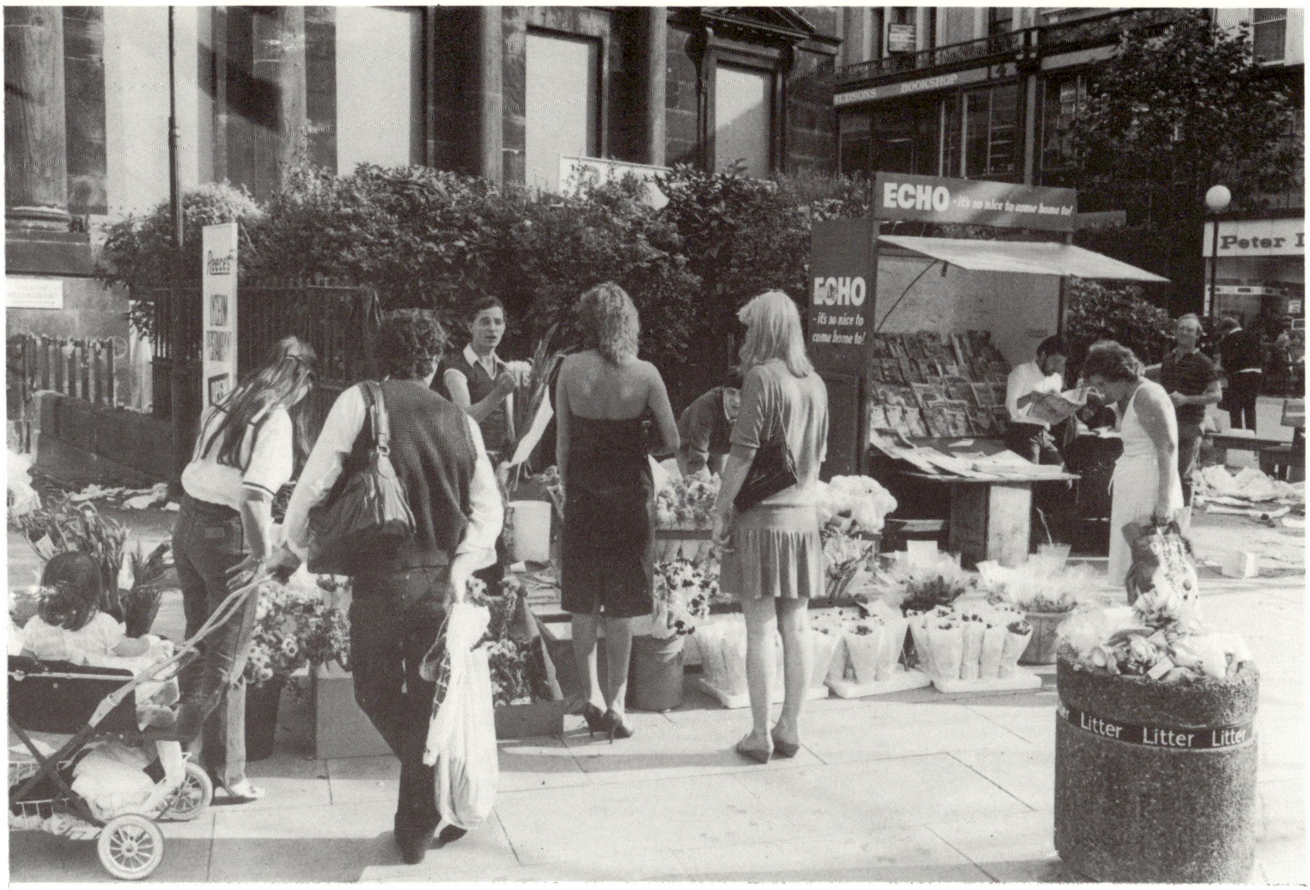
ECHO - it's so nice to come home to!
ECHO
- it's so nice to come home to!
Litter Litter Litter

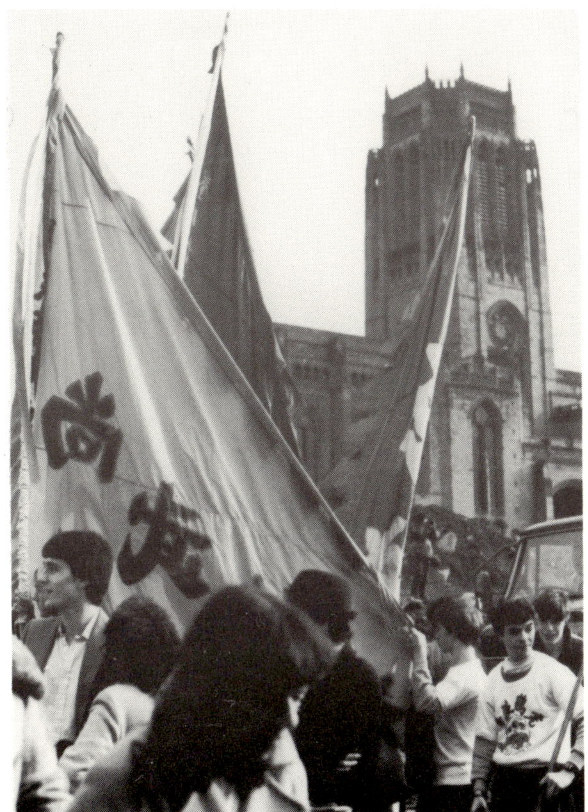

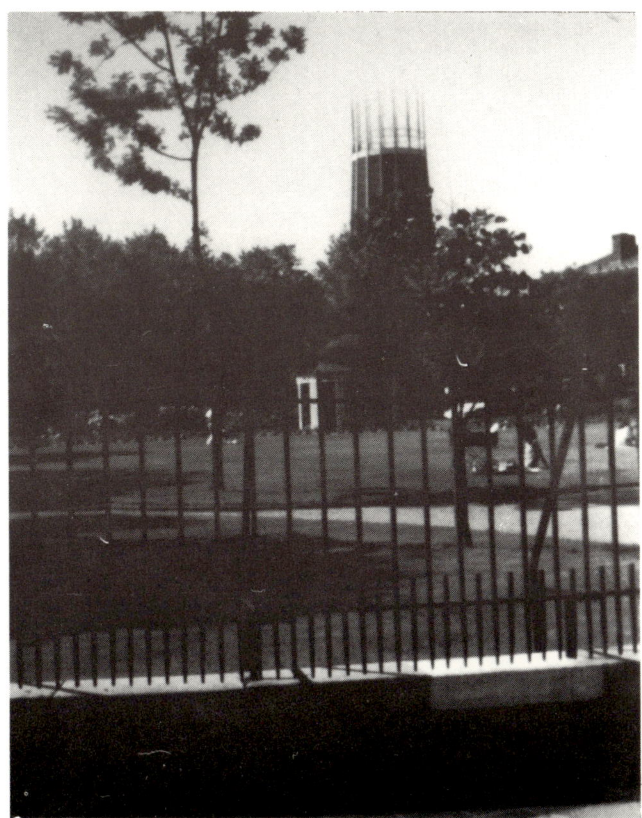

Shop window models — stiff, elegant limbs,
taut lines, false hair, fixed faces —
when they are left lying sideways
on the floor in *rigor mortis,*
or stripped naked to reveal mock breasts,
attain a certain pathos, repel the eye
like the helpless sick in hospital beds
you walk past discreetly to the one you know.

At Gateacre

Umber is the night
where the city warms the sky
and here a spirit moves
in the unharvested barley
beneath the skirted moon :

it moves unseen
in the monkgowned woods —

is there, is everywhere
in all the leaves of night
with their stilled singing.

The ridge grows short
in the lengthening dark
where the hill comes down,
inevitably down
into these fields, quiet,
enfolding, as in Leonardo's dream
of earth and womb,
tide and pulse.

Last Long

Last long
lingering loveliness
of this year's going:
go gently,
tinged with tenderness,
grass greying, growing.
Songs of the sparrows
sweeten still
the blurred and sepia scene —
branched in the dying light
until
there are leaves
where leaves have been.

And you, my love
are as new to my loving
as the leaves are old
upon the wistful bough;
and our song carries
the rare, burgeoning pathos
of the sparrows
in a winter city.
O love,
last long.

Ithaca-Liverpool

My father came today: an awaited visit,
the walk beachwards. Unusually quiet, he paced
the sand near the tide's persistent reach,
looking to the horizon broken by one dark ship.
'Like North Africa' he said suddenly. 'The war.
Thought I'd never return. I used to watch
from the shore, as from a desert island,
the convoys passing endlessly
carrying soldiers to who knows what.'
His eyes held the distance; in their deep grey
was a lost boy, an Odysseus never getting home.
When the war ended, his plane approaching
English cliffs turned back, defeated by fog;
like a great gull banking, it landed at Paris —
a city he never asked to know. Even now,
haunted in dreams, he sees them,
the ghost ships passing silently, one by one.

Ballad of the White Slave and the Brown

Two slaves in ships from Liverpool:
    One was white, one was brown.
The white one sailed from his home town,
    The brown from far Garoul.

The white slave was a ten year child,
    The brown a man one score —
The child captive for being poor,
    The man for his dark hide.

In Liverpool the boy was taken
    For a rich merchant's use:
Apprenticeship a dire abuse
    In a large plantation.

In Africa, for muskets, hats,
    Chintz, brandy, calico,
The trader's price a prime negro
    Tossed in the hold with rats.

West to Virginia both were sent,
    For tobacco exchanged —
One indentured, the other chained
    And never home they went.

Two slaves in ships from Liverpool:
    One was white, one was brown.
The white one pined for his home town,
    The brown for far Garoul.

P. P. Burdett del.

E. Rooker sculpt.

A View of the Custom House. Taken from Traffords Wyent.

Song of an L.P. *(to Bryan Blundell, founder of the Blue Coat School, 1718)*

I have L.P. branded on my arm in red.
My parents died of chincough and consumption.
Liverpool Pauper: I'm among the many
destitute, homeless and without a penny.

But today I leave my friends in this big Workhouse —
old Sam, Molly and little blind Fred.
I've been chosen for the Blue Coat School,
I'll wear a uniform, obey the rule,
learn to read and write and say my prayers —
for a few years, at least, relief from my cares.

By Victorian Moonlight *(Atkinson Grimshaw's Paintings of Liverpool)*

All those scenes by moonlight, with docks,
horse-drawn cabs, wet cobbles, the drizzle
just ceased — or beginning; people in cloaks
under the ghastly lamps, the murky glow.
Shop windows are crowded, lit like churches;
mothers and daughters cross the dusky street,
a desultory dog sniffing. Poultry hangs
(feathered pairs in rows), jewellery next door,
an ironmonger's sign, a draper's store.
Figures merge in distance, fade;
tasselled shadows, newspaper rags,
a sense of black railings,
the moon never seen.

All those atmospheric skies, tall ships
their rigging romantic in half-light.
The Quay, Wapping Dock, the Old Customs House
where cabmen hunch on carriages in mud,
tracks glistening: illusory gold
imbued by a moon just out of view.
Christmas, it seems, is close:
street vendors try their chance —
at any corner Her Benny might emerge
selling matches in the gloom.

All those scenes are plangency in paint,
preserving a picture,
putting a frame around Victorian Times.

The Coming in of Ancestors

Here are the strangers with shabby holdalls
and pale enigmatic smiles:
they disembark, looking around uncertainly
as cloud shadows move
on the moving Mersey;
and what they bring
is partly left at terminals;
and what they say
is scarcely comprehended.

Here are the docks, alive with arrivals,
cargoes of Irish, Germans, Poles.
Are they prepared
for what this land will give?
Will they, the foreigners,
ever feel they belong?
Perhaps not until their blood is passing
in the veins of English grandchildren.

My grandfather merges now
in the whisper of their lives:
his Scandinavian father
that whiskered man at chess
in the old, newly discovered photograph,
naturalised and with suitably altered name —
did he, as he slowly moved the chess pieces,
recall the forests, the fiords, the frozen winters?

My grandmother remembers her own:
Italian, in black toque hat,
wearing bright carnelian beads.

Here is their Liverpool —
the landfall in the west,
waterfront, heartland, home.

The Ballad of Everton Brow

(for my maternal grandparents,
John and Elizabeth Manlond)

Grass has returned
to Everton Brow :
gypsies and donkeys
are grazing there now.
Where are the pubs, the cellars, the entries,
the cracked stone step
where the great ones sat?
Where are the bins and the long barbed walls
that pricked and cut the unwary cat?
Where are the bubbles of tar in the street
glinting fragments of glass in the heat?

Weeds have returned
to Everton Brow :
blocks of cement
are growing there now.

Behind the white face of pristine stone
they sit white-faced
they sit alone;
eight storeys up (it could be eighteen)
at their particular window
in their own cement cell,
they stare at the glass
catching sun, catching rain,
recall eighty years
some with love, some with pain.
They don't come down
to break their bones.
They talk of the war — the last but one —
and the first baby born
(they had wanted a son).

Married before the breaking of war
they met on a ferry boat
(he winked and smiled),
the Mersey flowed
like their lovetide.

He was sent to the trenches
— a shrapnel scar —
he grew long whiskers
to hide the war.
Thought I was Kruger (he says) —
she says she waited
under the clock
at Lime Street Station — his train
was late, returning from Flanders
the mud, the hate.

Baby in arms
(the pram was to hold six more)
cows for the abattoir
passed the door.

Now they sit high up ('near the sky')
the city ebbs and flows below
a changing landscape sprawls beneath,
they've got central heating
it's clean, it's neat:
but the lifts are too small
to get a coffin in
to get a coffin out.

Grass has returned
to Everton Brow:
gigantic gravestones
have grown there now.

VPwine
VPwine

At the Poultry Stall *(Old St. John's Market)*

Christmas fever. Breath in the air.
Feathers. Gold glitter. At the Empire
the Principal Boy's a woman
with 'the longest legs in Show Business',
plump thighs in high boots. Purple velvet.

For the annual turkey-buying
my father takes me by the hand:
we pass the puppies in their market cages,
push through to the poultry stall;
then hours, it seems, of cogitation
on the merits of this or that bird
up on the marble counter, seasonal high altar.
I try not to see the awful offal
flung by raw hands, the reddened sawdust.
"These are dressed turkeys" my father explains.
"But they're undressed" I insist, frowning
at the bare plump bodies, floured for whiteness,
leg feathers left like fluffy boots.

Everything stops for the glamorous lady
arrived to purchase a pair of pheasants.
People press forward, nudging and peering;
the Principal Boy smiles down at me:
"What lovely golden curls" she murmurs.
I stare up at the fur-swathed, powdered woman,
imagine the longest legs in Show Business —
plump thighs topped by purple feathers.

The Cuttings

On all my rail journeys out from Lime Street
I've never missed the cuttings
never failed to be excited
by the dark high walls
the blackened sandstone
bedrock of the city, cut into
blasted, shaped by nineteenth century
enterprise. Steam, diesel, electric:
countless trains have slipped out
through these tall passes,
with human freight
each to an individual fate.

And mine: child pleasures first
bound for the London adventure,
secure in parents and a sense of history.
Later, the sad leavetakings,
aware now of personal destiny
the inevitable passage of each of us alone
out through a dark gorge.

On a cobbler's shelf sit signs
of the struggle and surge of existence.
Styles and shapes yield significance,
suggest the mould of lives.

And those shoes preserved through the ages,
glass-cased and labelled —
thonged Roman sandals, leather like liquorice,
paste buckles of late rococo,
ice-skates worn by Wordsworth,
Charlotte Brontë's bird-thin slippers —
poignant portrayals of invisible wearers.

In a throw-away age, this Garston shop
is a survivor too, like its cobbler:
a pre-war craftsman, anecdotal,
gnarled, on the last.

Over the Water

The Pond, West Kirby Cliffs

The pond on the cliff has returned.
Through morning curtains I saw the gleam —
water catching the eastern light
clouds in a mirror in mud.
The pond has returned, and returning
mocks the machines, builders' outriders.

Wild the cliff, humpy the ground
a wasteland with ragged daisies,
the pond deep-centred, jagged.
That's how it was. Now the land's flattened
filled in, rolled out like lumpy pastry
ready for raw, rising structures.
I remember one swampy spring
when unaccustomed heat
vapoured the cliffs after rain,
the frogs rose in their masses,
simmered, leapt like court jesters,
overflowed the bacchanalian pond,
flopped round our gardens.
Many were squashed under car wheels,
burst like pods, flattened like cartoon cats
only to rise again to roundness
in the shape of countless kindred
whose eyes baled at dusk, thousands of them,
threatening the estate, ready to avenge,
throats pulsating, croaks uniting
in a twilight chorus.

The pond on the cliff has returned.
Not for long. A house will be cemented
over the place of springtime sex and spawning.
Concrete floors, foundations, walls.
But on moon-lost nights will an insideous croaking
be heard? And will a thousand bulging eyes
haunt the corners of the rooms?

From Hilbre Island

Dissolution of day
on the estuary;
night's vast advance
on the evening tide;
and I, rock-lichen, cling
listening to sea-distance,
the murmur of a harmony
within a greater harmony

while from the fretted shore
humanity emits
a thousand brutish sounds
diffused and lost:

as on a distant plain
the sound of centuries repeats
and noise of conflict boils
from blue-skinned warriors
or scaly knights who swarm
like early amphibians
floundering, sea-emerged.

New Year's Eve

Shake of stars and frost shine
clear darkness
dilating in the eye of night
as the year shrinks
to the hooting of a ship's owl,
fog call of the far-off,
bark of death's dog,
enigmatic chiming of the mystery clock
and auld lang syne
wrung from the tilting throat
of present life
doomed to spin
in a mote of time.

And the cold moon staring
at old earth travelling, turning
travelling on:

the eye in the maelstrom
eternally drowning.

A child cries Mother!
Father!

Across the Mersey

mid-winter city glitter
icicle lights
wind scalpel-keen
cutting up from the cold coast
the grey Irish Sea its Celtic song
uncurling eternal lament
or exaltation

The International Garden Festival

This is a city surviving modern blitz and fire-bombs
and the battered image broadcast.

This is a cradle of nations still echoing
with sea-twinings of its once powerful Port.

This is a great garden of the nations
created on its rejuvenated shore.

Here are the hills scooped from silt,
salt wind in the leaves and flowers.

Here are the fabled birds, anchored high,
with green growth in their beaks.

Here is the river shining intermittently
hinting the resilience of its city.

Here is the sound
of a new sea-page turning.

List of Photographs and Photographers